BUDGERIGARS

AND

COCKATIELS

HOW TO KEEP, FEED AND BREED THEM

BY

C. P. ARTHUR

British Library Cataloguing-in-Publication Data
A catalogue record for this book is available from the
British Library

CONTENTS

HOW TO KEEP, FEED AND BREED THEM............... 1

AVICULTURE... 1

BUDGERIGARS 7

BUDGERIGAR BREEDING FOR BEGINNERS 27

BLUE BUDGERIGARS... 31

THE COCKATIEL.. 42

THE COCKATIEL - HOW TO BREED, TAME,
AND TEACH TO TALK 49

Aviculture

'Aviculture' is the practice of keeping and breeding birds, as well as the culture that forms around it, and there are various reasons why people get involved in Aviculture. Some people breed birds to preserve a specific species, usually due to habitat destruction, and some people breed birds (especially parrots) as companions, and yet others do this to make a profit. Aviculture encourages conservation, provides education about avian species, provides companion birds for the public, and includes research on avian behaviour. It is thus a highly important and enjoyable past time. There are avicultural societies throughout the world, but generally in Europe, Australia and the United States, where people tend to be more prosperous, having more leisure time to invest. The first avicultural society in Australia was The Avicultural Society of South Australia, founded in 1928. It is now promoted with the name Bird Keeping in Australia. The two major national avicultural societies in the United States are the American Federation of Aviculture and the Avicultural Society of America, founded in 1927. In the UK, the Avicultural Society was formed in 1894 and the Foreign Bird League in 1932. The Budgerigar Society was formed in 1925.

Some of the most popular domestically kept birds are finches and canaries. 'Finches' are actually a broader category, encompassing canaries, and make fantastic domestic birds, capable of living long and healthy lives if given the requisite care. Most species are very easy to breed, and usefully do not grow too large (unlike their larger compatriot the budgerigar), and so do not need a massive living space. 'Canary' (associated with the *Serinus canaria*), is a song bird is native to the Canary Islands, Madeira, and the Azores – and has long been kept as a cage bird in Europe, beginning in the 1470s. It now enjoys an international following, and the terms *canariculture* and *canaricultura* have been used in French, Spanish and Italian respectively, to describe the keeping and breeding of canaries. It is only gradually however (a testament to its growing popularity) that English breeders are beginning to use such terms. Canaries are now the most popular form of finch kept in Britain and are often found still fulfilling their historic role of protecting underground miners. Canaries like budgies, are seed eaters, which need to dehusk the seed before feeding on the kernel. However, unlike budgerigars, canaries are perchers. The average life span of a canary is five years, although they have been known to live twice as long.

Parakeets or 'Budgies' (a type of parrot) are another incredibly popular breed of domestic bird, and are originally from Australia, first brought to Europe in the 1840s. Whilst they are naturally green with yellow heads and black bars on the wings in the wild, domesticated budgies come in a massive variety of colours. They have the toes and beak typical of parrot like birds, as in nature they are climbers; budgies are hardy seed eaters and their strong beak is utilised for dehusking seeds as well as a climbing aid. When kept indoors however, it is important to supplement their diet of seeds with fresh fruit and vegetables, which would be found in the wild. Budgies are social birds, so it is most important to make sure they have company, preferably of their own kind. They do enjoy human companionship though, and may be persuaded, if gently stroked on the chest feathers to perch on one's finger. If not kept in an aviary, they need a daily period of free flight, but great care must be taken not to let them escape.

Last, but most definitely not least, perhaps the most popular breed of domestic bird, is the 'companion parrot' – a general term used for *any* parrot kept as a pet that interacts with its human counterpart. Generally, most species of parrot can make good companions. Common domestic parrots include large birds such as Amazons, African Greys, Cockatoos, Eclectus, Hawk-headed Parrots and Macaws; mid-sized birds such as Caiques, Conures, Quakers, Pionus, Poicephalus, Rose-Ringed parakeets and Rosellas, and many of the smaller types including Budgies, Cockatiels,

Parakeets, lovebirds, Parrotlets and Lineolated Parakeets. The *Convention on International Trade in Endangered Species of Wild Fauna and Flora* (also known as CITES) has made the trapping and trade of all wild parrots illegal, because taking parrots from the wild has endangered or reduced some of the rarer or more valuable species. However, many parrot species are still common; and some abundant parrot species may still be legally killed as crop pests in their native countries. Endangered parrot species are better suited to conservation breeding programs than as companions.

Parrots can be very rewarding pets to the right owners, due to their intelligence and desire to interact with people. Many parrots are very affectionate, even cuddly with trusted people, and require a lot of attention from their owners. Some species have a tendency to bond to one or two people, and dislike strangers, unless they are regularly and consistently handled by different people. Properly socialized parrots can be friendly, outgoing and confident companions. Most pet parrots take readily to trick training as well, which can help deflect their energy and correct many behavioural problems. Some owners successfully use well behaved parrots as therapy animals. In fact, many have even trained their parrots to wear parrot harnesses (most easily accomplished with young birds) so that they can be taken to enjoy themselves outdoors in a relatively safe manner without the risk of flying away.

Parrots are prey animals and even the tamest pet may fly off if spooked. Given the right care and attention, keeping birds is usually problem free. It is hoped that the reader enjoys this book.

BUDGERIGARS.

BUDGERIGARS

THEIR BREEDING AND MANAGEMENT.

By C. P. Arthur.

———

Budgerigars have become so popular in this country, as well as on the Continent, that a thorough treatise on their management will probably be accept able to the many hundreds who now keep these deservedly favourite birds. Their popularity is no doubt due not only to their lovely colours and markings, but to their readiness to nest and rear a numerous progeny in confinement, either in cage or aviary.

They are now bred in a number of colour varieties including yellows, blues, cobalts, whites, olive-greens, apple-greens and jade-greens. A "Silver-wing" variety has also been produced.

These birds have been known by many names in the past, such as Zebra Parrakeet, Undulated Parrakeet, Warbling Grass Parrakeet, etc. The Budgerigar seems to be the name that is now most popular. This is evidently a corruption of "Betcherrygah," the name the Australian Aborigines call them, meaning "Pretty Bird"; the Colonists, I believe, mostly call them "Canary Parrots."

They are found chiefly on the large grassy plains of Australia, feeding on the flowers and seeds of the long grasses. Their breeding places are chiefly in the southern parts, but if it is a dry season and their food is scarce they emigrate northwards, breeding in holes in decayed tree trunks, into which they burrow like rats, hundreds of pairs sometimes nesting in the same tree.

Budgerigars average from 7 inches to 7½ inches long; some birds, but few, measuring 8 inches. All the underparts and rump are bright grass green; the back, up to the crown of the head, greenish-black, each feather being edged with bright yellow. The flight feathers are more olive green on the outer edges, the third up to the eighth or ninth feathers having a white bar on them about half-way up, which does not show on the closed wings. The forehead and throat are bright yellow. A patch of turquoise blue appears on each cheek, with a black spot at the bottom of it, and four other black spots form a necklace round the throat. The two central tail feathers are blue; the others are dark green at the base and tip, but the central part of the feathers is brilliant yellow.

THE SEXES AND HOW TO
DISTINGUISH THEM.

The sexes are distinguishable chiefly by the cere at the base of the upper mandible, which in the male is always dark indigo blue after it is about four months old. In the female the colour of the cere varies very much, but is never dark blue. In the young of both sexes the cere is flesh colour, with a bluish tinge; the young cock gets darker blue, but the hen turns buffish.

When not in breeding condition, many hens turn quite blue on the cere; still never dark blue like the cock. I once had a hen which reared three nests of fine young ones, but her cere remained light blue the whole of the season. But as a rule the hen's cere turns from buff to brown when breeding, and will form quite a brown scale on the cere which peels off at the end of the season, often leaving the "nose" quite blue, but not dark blue.

I should like readers to bear this in mind, that the cere of a cock bird is always dark blue and never light blue, and a hen may as often be light blue as brown, but is never dark blue. This has caused a lot of confusion in the past (as I daresay some of the large importers and dealers have found), owing to some writers merely stating that the cere of the cock was blue and the hen brown.

9

SOME CURIOUS TRAITS.

Budgerigars will often live to a good old age. I knew of two cocks which lived together in a Canary's "hang-up" cage for 22 years. These were some of the importation of 1879. Over 50,000 pairs were imported into England during the first six months of that year, when they were sold at a guinea a dozen. But they were nearly all cocks; I had several dozen and there was not a hen amongst them.

These birds seldom drink in their wild state, getting sufficient moisture from the unripe grass seeds, and no doubt sipping the dew off the grass. People used to keep them without water, but I am glad to say this fad has completely died out. Still, it is an undoubted fact that they will live without water for a friend and schoolmate of mine brought several home from Australia a few years ago, and when he was leaving this country again for Australia asked me to have them. When I was bringing them away from his house, he told me not to give them any water. I told him I certainly should, as all mine drank. He assured me that they had not tasted a drop of water since he left Australia with them eighteen months before.

Mr. Wiener states that "cage-bred Undulated Parrakeets never acquire the bright green of their imported parents, and are found to breed less freely." I cannot tell whether, Mr. Wiener wrote this from hearsay or experience. If the latter, it is altogether contrary to my experience, and I have bred Budgerigars now for 25 years. Many years my season's young have numbered over five hundred, and my experience is that aviary-bred birds are much larger and quite equal in colour to imported birds, and also breed much more freely.

When it is borne in mind that their natural breeding season corresponds to our winter, it stands to reason they must be in this country at least twelve months before any breeding results can be expected. Besides, newly-imported Budgerigars are always very wild, banging themselves about the cage or aviary at the slightest movement of anyone near, making themselves quite a nuisance, in fact, to people inclined to be a bit nervous. I should certainly advise anyone intending to take up with this interesting hobby to leave the imported birds to those with large outdoor aviaries, and go in for tamer, aviary-bred birds.

NESTS AND BREEDING.

If cage breeding is intended, the larger the cage the better; I should say not less than 3ft. long, 2ft. high and 12 ins. deep. This would accommodate two pairs, for which four nests would be required. The best kind of nest for Budgerigars is the husk which the cocoa-nut comes out of. It is made by cutting a hole in the upper part of the pointed end and securely wiring the whole together, at the same time fixing some wires in the husk with which to hang it in place. It should be hung almost horizontally, the hole end a little elevated. In my aviaries I have tried every imaginable way of wiring, and with the hole at every part of the husks, and I found the birds discarded all except the ones with the hole at the end.

We will now suppose you have your cage and four husk nests. Hang the nests two at each end, close to the top of the cage, with a roost running about an inch from the front of the husk. It would be best in this case to put each pair in a small cage by themselves for a fortnight, to get paired, before turning them into the breeding cage. It may save squabbles, although these birds seldom fight, except over the husks. When two hens take a fancy to the same husk, they will fight like demons, and in the springtime I have frequently to go into my aviaries and separate hens on the floor, for they will fasten on to each other and then drop to the ground, and there fight it out like two cats, both often being covered with blood before the battle is over.

The hens lay from four to six white eggs (sometimes as many as eight or nine, but usually about six), which are laid on alternate days. The hen frequently commences to sit with the first egg, consequently there is a matter of ten or twelve days' difference in the ages of the young. But the hen is careful to look after the feeding of the last-born, and it is rarely anything goes wrong with it. They sit about twenty days, but I think in very hot weather the eggs hatch out a day or two earlier.

Mr. Gedney says in his book: "The young do not leave their nesting-place until fully fledged, which stage they attain when about fourteen days old, and at the expiration of another week they discard their parents and scratch for themselves." A writer in a Fancy journal a few years ago made the same statement, evidently copied from Gedney's book, as any breeder of Budgerigars knows perfectly well that young Budgerigars at fourteen days old are quite helpless, and almost naked, and are not feathered fit to leave the nest until they are at least five weeks old. I make a rule of leaving the family with the parent birds until the young ones' tails are full length, and, unless for hand-rearing, it is not safe to separate them from their parents before.

HOW TO FEED.

Canary and white millet seeds are the chief articles of diet, although the birds will relish a few white oats or a spray of millet. All kinds of things have been recommended for them when they have young, but I have proved they will rear good strong young on dry seeds alone. A mixture consisting of two parts canary seed, one part Indian millet, and one part white millet will be found satisfactory. The packet seeds offered by firms of repute such as those advertising in this book can also be relied on.

As I have said, the Budgerigar in its wild state lives mainly on the ripening seeds of grasses and will generally consume green food eagerly in captivity. A regular supply of seeding grass, groundsel, chickweed and similar food should be provided. See that the grass is seeding and not merely in flower. The latter has little food value. Take care that no frosted greenstuff is offered.

When the young leave the nest, a little scalded Canary seed should be given. This is better than letting them be confined to the hard seed. The seed should have boiling water poured over it at night, and be strained through a cloth in the morning, after it has been in soak all night. This must not remain in the aviary or cage long enough to get sour.

When putting up your birds for breeding, do not forget to provide them with plenty of cuttlefish bone, also give plenty of coarse, gritty sand. To those who have the opportunity, breeding these birds in an outside aviary is far better than cage breeding, although a lady I knew bred thirteen young Budgerigars from one pair of old ones in one season in an open wire cage, about 3 feet by 2 feet, containing also Java Sparrows, Waxbills, Saffron Finches, and others,

FITS AND EGG BINDING.

I will now jot down as they occur to my mind a few things likely to crop up at times in a breeder's experience. First of all, Budgerigars are very liable to drop dead in a fit, in the Spring more than at any other time of the year; I think this must be through being deprived of green food so much throughout the Winter. Anyway, I find it a very good plan as the Winter is passing over to give, if green food is short, a little Epsom Salts in the drinking water occasionally: This must be given in a glass or china (not metal) vessel, and in just sufficient quantity to make the water taste of it.

Sometimes the bird will recover from the fit, leaving it paralysed in one or both feet. When this is so, Budgerigars will sometimes recover, but in most cases they have another attack and then "take their ticket." When a bird is found to be paralysed, the only thing to be done is to put it into a small box cage with some scalded seed on the bottom, and give in a very shallow vessel some water with a little liquid magnesia in it, letting the bird remain perfectly quiet.

Another thing the breeder will be sure to be troubled with if he puts his birds up outdoors too early—which a few warm sunny days in March are sure to tempt him to do—is having egg-bound hens. To prevent this as much as is possible, give a plentiful supply of cuttlefish, and do not pair up your birds until April. When it does occur, some hens die in the nest, and there is no help for this, as you cannot search all the husks daily. Most hens, when egg-bound, however, will be on the floor of the aviary, and must be taken out at once, or the cock is sure to worry them.

After taking her out, get your little oil-can belonging

to your bicycle and just dip it into hot water to warm the contents. Then take the hen in the left hand, tail between the thumb and forefinger, head held securely with the little finger. And don't forget that an egg-bound hen Budgerigar can bite; if you forget she will probably remind you of it. The back of the bird should be towards your palm. Then push the tail back with your left thumb, insert just the tip of your tiny oil-can into the vent, and squeeze it sufficiently to force out just a few drops of the warm oil. Be careful not to overdo it. Then put the hen in a small box travelling cage with seed and water on the bottom, and keep her in a warm place.

This treatment will often relieve her, although she may not lay for a day or two. But if she seems very far gone, don't wait for more than a few hours after the oiling, but hold her vent over a small jug of hot water, trying the latter with the back of your hand first, to see that it is not too hot. After she has been steamed, if she does not soon lay, I hold her in my hand as before, and place the thumb and forefinger of the right hand on each side of her vent, and very gently press. She will at once feel the help, and though apparently so far gone as to be insensible, will at once begin to strain to relieve herself of the egg. After two or three "strains" you will see the white egg appear, as just a little white spot.

You must have a friend or helper with you then, possessed of a steady hand, and a small needle. Both your hands, of course, are occupied, and if you leave off the pressure of the

16

thumb and finger the hen will stop straining and the egg will go back. Get your helper to prick the egg with the blunt, or eye end, of the needle, being careful to prick nothing but the egg. This will let out the contents, and the shell will collapse and come away without further trouble. A hen which has been through this process should be kept by herself for a week. Continental breeders recommend pure cod liver oil mixed with the canary seed fed to the birds—two teaspoonsful to 3½ pints of seed—as a preventive of egg-binding.

DEFICIENCIES OF PLUMAGE.

Very often after the second round of nests, it will be found that young ones are leaving the nests without their long flight or tail feathers, but with the whole of the body and head perfectly feathered. This I believe to be caused not by in-breeding, as some say, but rather by over-breeding—that is, when the parent birds are beginning to get exhausted. I never discard these young ones, for the father of my Lutino Budgerigars, pure yellow with pink eyes, which I once bred, never had any long flight feathers for years, although his progeny were always perfectly feathered.

The best thing to do with these misfeathered youngsters is to put them into a large cage, wired only in the front, with the roof low down. Keep plenty of sawdust on the bottom to prevent them injuring the end joint of their wings when trying to fly, and as the moulting season comes on, buy some sulphate of iron. Instead of putting a little lump in the water, as is often recommended, put it in a clean, old jug, and pour some boiling water over it and stir up. When cold, pour off the solution into a bottle for use. A few drops of this in the drinking water (just sufficient to tinge it) well stirred up, is far better than putting a lump in the birds' water and leaving it to dissolve after the birds have drunk.

It will be found that most birds minus tails and flights will come all right at the moult under this treatment. Or Squire's chemical food may be used for the same purpose, but this is much more expensive.

It is often the case that before one nest of young are out of the husk the hen has commenced laying again; consequently the eggs get very much fouled by the excrément from the young. In this case you will need a teaspoon, a small hog's-hair brush or bit of flannel, and a basin of hot water—not too hot, but so that you can comfortably bear your hand in it. With the spoon take the eggs out of the nest and put them in the water, taking care they do not roll out of the spoon. After soaking a few minutes in the water, the dirt will easily wipe off with the wet brush or bit of flannel. Let them dry and return them to the husk.

CURIOUS HISTORY OF THE LUTINOS.

Speaking of hot water reminds me of a curious thing which happened regarding my pair of pink-eyed Lutino Budgerigars, and which made me think I had discovered a way of producing Lutinos. But whether my action had anything to do with it I must leave scientists to say. Looking round the husks to see that all was going on right, I noticed in this particular husk—which was near the ground, as the cock could not fly well—three eggs, two of which were quite covered with excrement from the last nest of young. As I knew the hen had commenced to sit, I called to my wife to bring me out a basin of hot water and a spoon, which she passed into the aviary to me. I put the spoon into the husk and brought out the two eggs, which I dropped into the water.

My wife's attention for the moment was taken up with some other inmates of the aviary. She then happened to look round, and, seeing what I had done, instantly exclaimed: "Charlie, you will kill those eggs. The water was boiling when I brought it out." I whipped them out of the water at once, wiped them clean, and put them back into the nest, though never dreaming they would hatch. But they did. And, strange as it seems, those two eggs produced what I believe to be the only Lutino Budgerigars ever known !

I kept these birds for two years and both bred with greens,

19

but try as I would I could not get them to breed together. They were purchased by Miss Howison for something like ten pounds, at the Cheltenham Show, where they won me the cup for the best exhibit. When the late Mr. Joseph Abrahams afterwards saw them exhibited by Miss Howison at a show in London, he told me he would gladly have given me twenty pounds for the pair had he known they were Lutinos.

I am afraid to say how many eggs I have since spoilt in experiments, but. without producing any more Lutinos. I should like to know if the water being too hot was likely to have influenced the colour of the young.

RED MITES, CANNIBALS, AND CATS.

Breeders will sometimes find the husks get infested with red mite. In this case get some Pyrethrum powder, and with the small bellows sold to use with it, blow plenty of the powder into the nest. It will not hurt the young, only make them cough until the dust settles. But transfer them to a new husk as soon as possible, which, remember, must be hung in the same place.

Sometimes a hen turns out a perfect cannibal, first biting the skin, and stripping the skull-bone of her young ones bare; if not seen in time, indeed she will then chew them to rags. The culprit can always be identified, as she does not wash the evidence of her guilt from her face, which will be covered with blood. I think my remedy for this sort of thing is the best and quickest. I catch the offender, take her outside the aviary, where the ground is covered with large flagstones, and, lifting my hand as high as I can reach, I dash her to the stones with all my force. This is quicker than chloroform.

I have seen fanciers recommend, when birds (and animals as well) have any unpleasant trick, to "get rid of them." I think that means simply passing your own trouble on to someone else, which no straightforward fancier should dream of doing. I may add that if one of these cannibals be allowed to remain in the aviary after tasting blood, she will soon recommence operations on other young after her own are gone.

Anyone breeding Budgerigars out of doors must be careful to guard against cats. When I erected my first lot of aviaries I used only galvanised netting of half-inch mesh, thinking this would secure the birds against any cat. But as soon as the young began to leave the nests my troubles began.

For the first week or so after the young are out and about, their favourite roosting method at night seems to be to hang with the hook of the upper mandible to the wire netting, holding on as well with their feet. The cats see them, climb stealthily up the netting, catch hold of a foot with their teeth and pull until the leg comes away from the body. The bird seldom dies as one would think, but the blood and feathers dry over the wound, and the first thing you notice is that you seem to possess birds which must have been hatched with one leg, for after a few days there is not the slightest sign of their having ever had two.

The remedy for this state of things is double wire. The outside wire should be at least two inches away from the other, and $\frac{3}{4}$in. mesh will do well for it, besides being not so dear.

BREEDING BUDGERIGARS WILD

It has often been suggested that Budgerigars would do well wild in this country, seeing that they stand our winters so well out of doors. This has been tried, but proved a complete failure owing to their migratory instincts. The birds migrate from one part of the Australian Continent to the other, according to the grass season.

Some years ago, Captain Spicer, of Spye Park, who is a great lover of nature and birds especially, consulted me as to stocking his park with them. I thought it was a grand idea; that we should be able soon to claim the Budgerigar as a naturalised British bird. I supplied the captain with sixty pairs, all large, strong, aviary-bred birds, and with over a hundred wired husks, some of which were hung in a wired enclosure, and others about the house and park. As there is a large deer park round the house and several very watchful keepers, there was little fear of the birds getting shot or destroyed.

The sixty pairs were put into an open wire place where they

had room to exercise their wings and have a good look round at their surroundings. After about a fortnight a small door in the netting was let down, and they were allowed to go in and out at will, a good supply of seed being always kept in the aviary ready for them. They soon made themselves at home. Some nested in the old decayed trees about the park, but the majority seemed to prefer the husk nests that were provided for them.

All went on swimmingly, and when the first nest of young were out they appeared to be everywhere. Every one who heard of the experiment was delighted. But alas ! "The schemes of mice and men gang aft agley." When the Autumn came, although food in abundance was provided for them, all except about twelve pairs disappeared never to return. Those that remained the Winter through did well, and commenced breeding early in the following Spring. I had a young one, about seven weeks old, brought to be stuffed, which had been killed at the end of March about seven miles from Spye Park; so its parents must have nested successfully in mid-Winter.

All the birds seemed to do well and breed freely that Summer, but in the Autumn every bird disappeared this time, and I have not heard of a single specimen having been seen on the estate since. So if anyone else contemplates repeating the experiment he must be prepared to renew the stock every Springtime,

SOME CONCLUDING HINTS.

Young Budgerigars do. not get their yellow forehead until the first moult. Until then the pencilling on the head is continued from the crown down over the forehead. They get their yellow forehead when about six months old, and the sex can generally be told then.

Care must be taken to guard against in-breeding, or the stock will soon degenerate, and instead of being larger and better birds than imported specimens, they will come small, weakly and featherless, some being not much larger than a Siskin. Here is the best plan to adopt, supposing you have breeding room for fifty pairs:—

The importation of Budgerigars usually takes place in the Spring. If some good birds arrive from Australia, get 25 pairs of them. But be careful to examine their feet and claws to see that none are missing; also, be sure to keep them in quarantine for a few weeks to see that they are free from septic fever. Many of the Australian Parrakeets, Rosellas and Pennants especially, die off wholesale from this disease after arriving here (as I know to my cost), caused by overcrowding, dirty cages and foul water during the voyage.

When you have your 25 pairs of Australians, pick out all the cocks and put them with 25 of your own aviary-bred hens. Then put the Australian hens with your 25 aviary-bred cocks.

These will breed you young which you should be proud of; quite as good in colour as imported birds and much larger in size.

The yellow or mealy Budgerigars are no doubt produced chiefly by in-breeding; consequently they are not so hardy as the green ones. The late Mr. Abrahams told me he thought the yellows could be produced from greens in seven generations, but I think they are got from yellows cropping up now and again among the young. I have had them crop up two or three in a season, before I had any yellow birds in my aviaries.

Breeders should be careful not to have an odd, unmated hen in the aviary, as she will cause no end of mischief, turning out eggs, killing young ones, and quarrelling with the other hens. But an unmated cock or two seldom works any mischief in this respect.

Mr. Wiener says: "Talent for learning to talk the bird has none, but one or two authentic cases are recorded of Budgerigars learning to say a word or two, probably about as well as the talking seal (called talking fish) once exhibited in London." Now in spite of what Mr. Wiener says, I can assure readers that Budgerigars hand-reared from the nest have wonderful talent for learning to talk. I have had and sold some really fine talkers, as I have letters to prove. They quickly realised five pounds each, so, of course, they are not quite so plentiful as blackberries in Autumn. I have one now—about nine months old, a very distinct talker—more so than many

Amazon Parrots. He says: "Joey's a beauty," "Dear Joey," "Kiss pretty Joey," "Oh, you beauty," "Open the door, please," "Let Joey out," etc. There is no need to tell a listener what he is saying, as is often the case with Parrots.

Budgerigars must be hand-reared to become thoroughly tame, as they cannot be tamed by giving them tit-bits, like many other birds, for they refuse anything but seed. To hand-rear Budgerigars is a rather tedious task, as the seed must be scalded, soaked, and then shelled before giving it to the young birds, which should be taken from their parents when the tail is about an inch and a half long. They can then be accustomed to being carried about 01. the hand or head, and will fly from cage to finger, etc. Anyone who has a tame, hand-reared talking Budgerigar has one of the most delightful pets imaginable.

Should anything have been overlooked in this section on these favourite birds of mine that readers would like to know, a letter to "Cage Birds" will receive prompt attention and advice.

BUDGERIGAR BREEDING FOR BEGINNERS

By W. Laskey.

From a boy I was an admirer of the "little, long-tailed Love-birds," as they are called, but it was not until I permanently settled that I was able to indulge in that particular branch of the Fancy. I then discovered that breeding Budgerigars was not such an easy matter as I had been led to believe by people of theoretical experience. I read books, consulted men that professed to know how to breed anything and everything from an evenly-marked Canary to a tortoiseshell tom-cat. Some advised Continental bred birds, others freshly-imported Australian; some had one theory, some another; all agreed it was quite easy. But I met with very indifferent success until about eighteen or twenty years since.

I bought four pairs of aviary-bred birds from Mr. C. P. Arthur, and from that time until about two years since, when I found it necessary to clear for want of room, all went as merry as the proverbial cricket, and considering the little care and attention required, it is astonishing this interesting and

27

most remunerative branch of the Fancy has not become more popular.

Your first and most important point for consideration is good, healthy stock. Get a few pairs of good English aviary-bred birds from a reliable breeder, but be careful they are aviary-bred and not imported birds. There are tricks in all branches of the Fancy; therefore do not hesitate to pay a fair price, and see you get the right birds. Budgerigars do much better and breed more freely in an outside aviary in quantities of, say, from four to twenty pairs, providing, of course, you avoid overcrowding.

The size of the aviary must necessarily be left more for the consideration of the pocket. I prefer one, say, about 16 feet square, and about 12 feet in height at back, made in the form of a lean-to, closed in at back and sides, the roof to extend hall-way from the back, the remainder of the roof and front of aviary being wire, with half-inch wire netting. Although these birds rarely or never bathe, they will thoroughly enjoy sitting in a shower of rain in the Summer, and the rain water will do much to improve their plumage and help them in their moult.

An old hollow or decayed trunk of a tree will cause endless amusement both for the birds and their owner. The floor of the aviary should be covered with gravel which can be kept raked over, and a heap of old mortar should be kept in the corner for the birds to peck at. This is very necessary, especially during the breeding season.

Some breeders advocate a small hollow log in preference to the cocoanut husk. It certainly seems more natural, but I have always derived better results from using the husks. Care should be taken that in cutting the hole (whether it is on the top or end of the husk) that it is only just large enough for the hen to squeeze through, and after the pairs have chosen their husks and settled down, remove all spare ones, and do not on any consideration allow an odd hen with your breeding stock, or she will cause endless trouble to the other hens.

The sexes can be easily distinguished, the cock having a dark blue cere, and being more or less glazed at the top of the beak, whilst the hen has a pale brown cere, which becomes slightly corrugated at about the time she is ready to lay. The beginner will easily be able to tell by this when breeding operations are about to commence.

The hen lays on an average about six eggs. Incubation starts with the first egg, and as she only lays about one every other day, the birds hatched first are often a week old before the last one makes its appearance. Regardless of this, the older birds seldom, if ever, crush the younger. The hen will keep the nest scrupulously clean, but it is advisable to shake a little insect powder into the nest, as these pests are a great nuisance to the birds during the hot weather.

Do not attempt to take more than three mests during the

season; two are quite sufficient if your aim is to keep healthy stock. If you take three nests from them, select your stock birds from the first or second round. April will be found quite early enough to start breeding. Remove and burn the husks as soon as you have finished, for they will continue to breed as long as you leave the husks with them.

Remove the young ones to a separate aviary as soon as they are able to cater for themselves. Their staple food should consist of equal parts of good sound Canary seed and white millet, with a few good oats during the breeding season; beyond this they will not require any additional food for rearing their young. A bunch of grass when in seed will be appreciated, also a large turf of long grass, well watered, in which they will roll and gambol to their hearts' content.

BLUE BUDGERIGARS.

HOW TO PRODUCE THE CHOICEST SPECIMENS.

By allen silver

Blue Budgerigars can be managed exactly the same as the green or yellow forms in so far as food and accommodation are concerned.

Healthy stocks not too inbred or overworked are just as hardy and accommodating as their less expensive brethren, and in some cases under my notice where they have been successfully maintained and bred for years, stock birds have been subjected to exceedingly low, but dry, temperatures, without harm to themselves or their progeny.

As this form of Budgerigar is blue owing to a loss of certain things in its make-up, it is more essential to guard against too close in-breeding than is the case with the normal green bird.

In consequence, the introduction of equally hardy blood of the same colour or the inter-crossing with true blue-throwing greens or olives, are items which call for attention from time

31

to time.

There is a considerable difference in density of colour between the deepest form of Light Blue or Sky Blue Budgerigar and the Dark or Cobalt Blue variety.

Gradations in both these colours occur, and from an exhibition standpoint both are equally attractive.

DENSITY OF COLOUR MUST BE WATCHED.

It is, however, very essential that a limit of density of colour should be strictly adhered to in judging, otherwise the very charming original form of light blue may be supplanted by a bird that is all but a dark blue.

The main attraction of the blue form of Budgerigar is its comparative uncommonness and price.

I feel, however, that had blue been the original colour of this little Grass Parrakeet, instead of green, and green Budgerigars had came into being in the same way, they would have been hailed with equal enthusiasm.

Blue Budgerigars probably arose in the first instance in 1881.

Mons. J. Baily Maitre, writing in the "Avicultural Magazine" for October, 1925, refers to birds figured on a plate in 1882 which was executed from living examples owned by M. Limbosch, a Belgian, who is said to have preserved the strain with great care.

The chances are that it first occurred to its original breeder as a mutation like the Ancon ram, but, being an attractive sport, unlike the Ancon ram, it was safely guarded and encouraged, although its appearance in numbers was small for a long period.

Messrs. Blanchard, of Toulouse, in late years probably did more than any other commercial firm towards the production of Blues in quantity; so much so that in 1925 they were within reach of the comparatively poor.

THE REMARKABLE DEMAND FOR BLUES.

The curious and spontaneous demand with ever-increasing prices which arose between February, 1926, and February, 1927, made them very desirable to those by whom birds are mainly regarded as a source of living or investment.

Whether this astonishing demand will continue for long we have yet to learn. But the most gratifying result of it is that a greater interest in Budgerigars generally has sprung up, and also a great demand for Greens that might produce Blues.

Quite large prices were paid for reputed Blue-throwing Greens, some of which were very "plebeian" as to ancestry, and were about as likely to throw anything but their own colour as two pure green Canaries to throw a clear.

When one has to manage a colour variety in animals, it is interesting, and to an extent necessary, to try and understand something about heredity, the study of which is still in its infancy.

It is, however, encouraging to note that bird-keepers favouring Budgerigars are really trying to get a grasp of the subject, and are not content to keep to the chance methods adopted in other circles.

One must never dogmatise regarding experiments in relation to living things, but one can expect from the past and tried experience of others that certain results can be achieved.

Superficially, like is said to produce like, but, as a matter of fact, it does not, for each new organism produced varies in a seen or unseen way from its male and female parent and from its immediate brothers and sisters.

Thus each new living organism produced has a chance of, so to speak, giving birth to a new character or ability not previously exhibited by its ancestors.

On the other hand, it is well known that animals of a pure line, *i.e.,* pure bred, showing one marked peculiarity, say, of colour, when paired to a pure line possessing exactly the same character, produce young all exhibiting this character, the reverse being the case when pedigree is unknown.

COLOUR PIGMENTS IN BIRDS.

For instance, a pure line of Blue Budgerigars paired to a pure line of the same colour produce Blue young.

The Budgerigar has proved no exception to this rule, and experiments regarding the one character of colour carried out on Mendelian lines with sufficient material and sufficient care, have worked out in several instances exactly as expected.

But where no certified pedigree has been forthcoming, naturally doubts have arisen.

Blue as a colour pigment like green is unknown in birds. The only exceptional green pigment known is the extraordinary ferric pigment found in the plumage of the Plantain eaters called Turacoverdin.

Many feathers in birds representing iridescent metallic colours of a blue, ruby, purple flame or green hue, varying according to the degree of sunlight or position of the bird when viewed, simply convey such appearances on account of their structure.

A yellow extractable pigment known as Zooxanthin, however, is well known, and it is a coloured fatty oil.

It is a diffused pigment and it usually tinges the shafts, rami and radii of feathers and possibly the feet and bills of birds.

Zoomelanin is a black colouring matter found in birds and

other animals, and it is distributed in little corpuscles in a dense or diluted fashion.

Their entire absence or excess is responsible for an altered colour appearance or even an increase or loss of vigour in the animal itself.

HOW FEATHER COLOUR IS MADE UP.

The green colour appearance of feathers in parrots is always, I believe, due to yellow, orange or greyish-brown pigment, with a special super-structure.

Orange hues are produced by red pigment (Zoo-nerythrin) with a yellow super-structure.

Blue feathers contain only orange or brownish pigment, and these feathers appear blue almost always owing to certain fixed characters in their make-up.

Brown in birds is a result of a mixture of red and black colouring matter, and white is never due to any pigmentation at all.

The entire substance of a white feather, *i.e.,* its so-called ceratine, is without colour, but its network of texture diffracts and reflects light.

In white Pigeons descended from the wild Rock Dove, which possesses iridescent feathers on its neck, even the altered colourless white feathers in this region retain their peculiar structure which allows them still to remain faintly metallic.

The distribution of these colour pigments, their presence or absence, and an alteration in the superstructure of the feathers, are all matters which are closely allied to the causes of sportive variation in the case of the Budgerigar.

The natural allocation of colour pigment in areas presenting normally a yellow or green appearance, scalloped, lined or laced with black, etc., has in the blue-looking bird undergone a change, and owing to such changes feathers that looked green now appear blue, and feathers that appeared yellow, white.

As this attractive variation has become fixed, and Blue Budgerigars are desirable, naturally many people wish to possess and breed them, and one is continually asked by correspondents how to set about it.

PRACTICAL MATING ADVICE.

Provided one has the means to procure pairs of pure Blues, be they dark or light, blue young in satisfactory numbers are produced, and, as before mentioned, an introduction of equally healthy unrelated blood will ward off degeneracy.

Such strains can be maintained in vigour by pairing blues to greens, olives or yellows, and the progeny paired back to blues, the resulting young of the desired colour proving valuable sires and dams for future use.

A blue-bred green, yellow or olive is produced by pairing a blue or dark blue to a bird of these respective colours. But a bird bred from the pairing of two blue-bred greens or other added colour selected at random may not have blue throwing capacities at all.

Unless tested it may be a pure olive green or yellow in spite of ancestry, and not one of that percentage of young produced with blue throwing possibilities.

Provided sufficient material is available, and absolute certainty is observed regarding the history of agents used over a series of pairs employed, the results should work out as follows:—

Blues paired to pure greens produce green offspring, which are truly blue-bred greens, otherwise greens derived from blue and green crossing.

When such birds are paired to pure blues they should produce embryos which, if they live to emerge and develop so that they can be examined, will be found to be coloured blue in the proportionate average of 50 per cent., the remaining 50 per cent, being greens, which are truly blue-bred greens, or greens with a blue throwing capacity and of true blue derivation.

BREEDING FROM BLUE-BRED GREENS.

On the other hand, when two genuine, tested blue-bred

greens of the kind just described (*i.e.,* produced either from a pairing of green to blue, or resulting from a crossing of blue paired to blue-bred greens), are mated together, they should produce embryos which when mature should work out in the following proportion:—

Twenty-five per cent, pure blues, 50 per cent, greens of mixed parentage, *i.e.,* blue-bred greens with a possible blue throwing capacity when paired to blues, and 25 per cent, pure greens without blue throwing capacity, in other words, young which have reverted to the original green parent in colour throwing capacity.

These latter Greens are the source of much disappointment when sold as blue-bred Greens without a test, and I am afraid it is only by test they can be recognised.

By looking at them one is entirely at sea. I do know that certain known adult blue-throwing Greens have in artificial light appeared to be pure Blues with white faces, and in daylight the most normal-looking of Greens.

But I (should not place any reliance upon such appearance.

The ancestry of Olive blood may be recognised in some Greens, but regarding Blue ancestry in a Green, I should be loath to give any opinion from an external examination alone.

The microscopical and chemical examination of the plumage

of colour varieties in Budgerigars exhibits a distribution or absence of pigment and altered cellular structure which has been carefully explained in a lecture originally given in Bremen by Dr. H. Duncker, who worked in conjunction with Consul-General C. H. Cremer, both of whom are members of the Budgerigar Club.

This lecture has been published in book form.* It is written on scientific lines and will be readily understood and of considerable interest to those having an elementary knowledge of ornithology.

Their experiments have been confirmed to a degree in this country by Mr. Denys Weston, Mr. M. T. Allen, and others.

I regard their carefully considered work as being worthy of serious consideration, but I do not expect it to be possible for most people to work out the experiments on the same lines, owing to the great necessity for care coupled with the fact that many birds and plenty of accommodation for them will be found necessary.

I do, however, feel that those who are content to try and produce Blues from green birds described as blue-bred, but of unknown pedigree and untested, will meet only with disappointment.

* Obtainable from the publishers of this book. Price 1/-.

THE COCKATIEL.

THE COCKATIEL

HABITAT AND WILD LIFE.

Indigenous to Australia, breeding in the South, then migrating to the North, it is found in vast numbers. According to Gould, these birds are found breeding in the wooded flats of most of the rivers that flow to the North-West. He states he has seen the ground covered with them engaged in feeding on the seeds of mature grasses, etc., and that it was no uncommon circumstance to see them by hundreds on the dead branches of gum trees in the neighbourhood of water, which they frequently visit for the purpose of satisfying their thirst; comparing this with their similar practice in the aviary, it would appear that a constant supply of water is essential to keep them in health and condition. With the exception of the North-East corner of Queensland, they range practically over the whole of Australia. Quarrion is their native name; they are also known as the Crested Ground Parrakeet, and Grey and Yellow Top-knotted Parrot. But such names are seldom used either by dealers or aviculturists in this country.

PLUMAGE.

Adult male: The general body covering is an extremely chaste arrangement of grey and white, the contrasts of which are very striking, yet with an entire absence of harshness; this beauty of general plumage, its beautiful primrose-yellow cheeks, and its ear patches of brick-red, combine to make a really striking and handsome bird. The crest is mostly yellow, as are the cheeks; the top of head, neck, back, and wing are ashen-grey; there is a broad band of white from the shoulders over the greater wing coverts; the under parts are pale ashen-grey; tail, dark grey on its proper surface and blackish underneath; back, legs and feet, grey; iris, nut brown. Total length, 13in.; tail, 5½ to 6in.

SEXUAL DISTINCTION.

The female lacks the yellow cheeks of the male; hers being grey, lightly suffused with yellow; her ear coverts are greyish-red, those of the male being bright brick-red; her crest is entirely grey, that of the male being practically all yellow; the underside of her tail is regularly barred with grey, yellow and white, that of the male being dull black.

YOUNG.

These resemble the adult hen, but are a trifle greyer, and their plumage lacks the bloom of adults. At the first moult they come into adult plumage, and cannot then be distinguished from their parents. The primrose-yellow cheeks of the males increase slightly in intensity of colour with each successive moult; this is also the case with the females, the yellow suffusion on their cheeks being much stronger on old birds than on those of, say, two years old.

They are quite blind for the first five or six days, and covered with longish yellow hairs; they soon grow, are ugly masses of pin feather at from six to fourteen days old, and are fully fledged at about three and a half weeks old (it is very difficult in a large aviary with these birds to tell their age to a day or two, as with the large amount of noise going on, the faint call of the young is almost drowned by the other aviary noises for the first few days). They leave the nest at four and a half to five weeks old, sometimes a little longer, though some writers give it as three or four weeks, but this has certainly not been my experience. They return to the nest for the first few nights, but soon settle down to roosting among the branches, and mostly in the open portion of their enclosure.

A keen observer can usually pick out the sexes even in their nest feather; in the males the front of the crest is lighter than

44

that of the females, and the observant aviculturist will soon learn to sort out the sexes when they are about six or seven weeks old, or even earlier.

BREEDING.

In their native haunts they nest in the spouts or hollow limbs of the gum trees, so common to Australian wilds. The bird fashions some cavity to its liking, and lays its clutch of three to five white eggs (1.2 by .9 in.) on the bare wood. Incubation takes from 16 to 17 days; both sexes take part in incubation, the male during the day and the female during the night. The season is from November to February, and two broods are usually reared.

In the aviary the best nesting receptacle is either a log (obtainable from any large dealer), or a small barrel hung up longitudinally, with a 3m. diameter hole cut in one end; these birds have a mind of their own, and will use it too, and mostly choose, when in a mixed series, any receptacle but the one put up for them, as I know to my cost; I have had one season practically nullified by their annoying stupidity in this respect; they have chosen flat-bottomed boxes, and nearly all the eggs have been spoiled by rolling about. This is one of the inconveniences of keeping a variety of birds together.

They do not attempt to breed till they are two years old, and even adult birds seldom breed the first year of their occupancy of the aviary, but usually they settle down to nesting seriously the following year, and keep merrily on, only stopping (not always, for I have had young reared during this period) for the moult. They seem more prolific in the aviary than in their native wilds, sometimes as many as seven being reared as a single brood.

As the hen begins to sit with her second egg, there is fully a week between the first and last hatch when the clutch is a full one, so the young emerge at intervals, but this seldom makes any difference, for all are usually reared, and often the first out assists in feeding his brothers and sisters. It is seldom, indeed, that any mishap occurs, for with the plenitude of food to hand, and immunity from the dangers common to all wild life in their native haunts, they are practically continuous breeders in the aviary; occasionally a pair turn up that lay eggs innumerable and seldom hatch one out. With such there is nothing to do but to get rid of them (turn them loose in some park) and secure another pair.

My first brood of young were reared entirely on Canary, millet, and greenstuff, but later they had access to soft food, oats, dari, sunflower, wheat, etc., and meal worms, and they helped themselves freely to all, as also do Budgerigars. When kept in an aviary by themselves let them have a pan of Canary and white millet, and another of wheat, dari, oats, and sunflower, with green food ad lib., just what happens to be in season; they are extremely fond of grass in flower,

A liberal supply of old mortar rubbish, crushed egg-shells, and cuttlefish must be kept up, or cases of egg-binding will be frequent. I have always attended to this, and have never had a case of egg-binding with this species. If a young male is taken as soon as it can feed itself, or better, as soon as it is fully fledged, and hand-reared, it makes a charming pet as a cage bird, and learns to speak a few words. I have seen such, but have not personally so experimented with them.

GENERAL NOTES.

This is the bird par excellence for the mixed series m an outdoor aviary, for with many years' experience of these charming birds I have never known them to snap at even the smallest occupant of their enclosure. If not clad in royal purple as some of their congeners, they are certainly not plain or dull coloured birds; my oldest male (10 years at least) is a handsome fellow, the grey and white contrast of his body plumage, brilliant yellow cheeks and red ear coverts making him one of the most striking birds in the aviary, even with Red Rosellas to keep him company. When moulting he never seems to have a feather out of place, and he has never had the slightest ailment all the years he has been in my possession. It is really a shapely bird of generally fine appearance, and is of a confiding and fearless demeanour.

My birds will permit me to do anything with them. Some actually let me pick them up. They will take their food on the ground close to my feet, so long as I keep still, and on the branches will not move when I am within six inches of them, only if I attempt to lay hold of them, then they will fly to another perch near at hand, and though I have many rare and valuable birds, very few of them are more interesting, In spite of their being now comparatively common, I should certainly not care to banish them from the aviary; though I must admit I should find them trying in the house. That is their one fault; they have a voice, and they believe in using it. At the same time, I am bound to say that I have never had any of my neighbours lodge any complaints concerning them, and I can with confidence recommend the Cockatiel as an interesting and entertaining pet, especially so for the garden aviary; and as they thrive even with the roughest treatment, the veriest tyro need not hesitate to try his 'prentice hand with them. Budgerigars are not safe with Finches, etc.; but the Cockatiel I have never found to harm even the smallest Waxbill, though I have kept the species on and off for over twenty years.

THE COCKATIEL

HOW TO BREED, TAME, AND TEACH TO TALK.

There can be but few fanciers who know what lovely and affectionate pets Cockatiels make when reared from the nest, or they would be much more popular than at present, for they are most easily bred and require very little attention compared with most other foreign birds. They are free breeders, will stand the coldest winter outdoors, are easily tamed, make free talkers, and will learn to whistle a tune more quickly than any bird I know.

Imported Cockatiels, like imported Budgerigars, seldom breed the first year they are in this country, being very wild, and it takes considerable time for them to settle down. Besides, their natural breeding season corresponds with our Winter. It is much the best plan to start with a good pair of aviary-bred birds; there are plenty to be got now. These would cost from £3 to £4 per pair, and would prove cheaper than half-a-dozen pairs of the cheap stuff so much advertised.

SEXING THE BIRDS.

Cockatiels are about twelve inches long, the tail accounting for about five inches. A slate grey is the predominant colour; the cock has a bright primrose-yellow face and crest, and a patch of bright red on each side, covering the ears. The hen has only a slight yellowish tinge on the face and a shade of red showing on the ears; but some hens get much brighter than others. Another distinguishing mark of the hen is the beautiful wavy lines of yellow on the under side of the tail. These lines run across, similar to the markings on a Pheasant's tail; but the outer feathers are sometimes all yellow. The young resemble the hen until the first moult. But even in the nests the young cocks have a bolder look, a fuller eye, and a more "bully" head than the hens.

One well-known writer on foreign birds has stated that Cockatiels have not the power of erecting or depressing the crest at will like the Cockatoos, but this is a mistake. If two Cockatiels show fight to each other, they will lay their crests down perfectly flat; then, if startled, the crest instantly goes up, erect as possible. Further, if you have a tame cock Cockatiel, and are fondling him, you will find the bird erects or lowers his crest according to the humour or temper he is in.

ROOM FOR BREEDING.

For breeding, an empty room with a window facing South will do very well for the purpose, but a place out of doors is greatly to be preferred. Anyone who has a small garden, or even a backyard, where there is plenty of sun, can erect in a few hours accommodation for a pair of Cockatiels. A place six feet high in front, if against a wall four or five feet long, and three or four feet from back to front, will be ample. Let it be weather-boarded on top and then tarred and thatched, or match-boarded and covered with corrugated iron. If boarded only, the sun splits the boards and so lets in the wet. Half the front may be board and half wire, and the door should be in the end where the boarding is, so that when you enter the birds will fly to the wire and not to the door through which you are entering. The door should be low, so that if the birds fly towards you when entering there will be wing space above your head.

ON BUYING BIRDS.

The next thing is to get your birds. An advertisement in "Cage Birds," stating fully your wants, will no doubt get you what you require; that is, if you do not know a breeder of these birds you can rely on. But, as I said before, don't go in for cheap birds, newly imported, or it is a hundred to one you will be disappointed. My first pair of Cockatiels I paid 30/-for, from Mr. C. W. Gedney, the popular and instructive writer on foreign birds; that was somewhere about thirty years ago. Now, £3 or £4 would be a fair price for a good pair of adult birds.

NESTING AND NEST BOXES.

Now we have our aviary up, and a pair of genuine aviary-bred birds in it, the next thing is to provide a suitable nest. Dr. Greene has recommended small barrels laid on their sides, with a hole at the end. I have tried them, but with indifferent success. I have also tried hollow branches, hollow logs, boxes with half a cocoanut husk fixed in, and also, as one writer recommends, a nesting-place made of bricks on the floor of the aviary. But none of my Cockatiels would ever look at a nest on the ground, and I have kept and bred some scores, and have, several pairs breeding at the present time.

All the above nesting-places have their advantages and disadvantages, but the nest I have found the most successful, and not only for Cockatiels, but also for such birds as Rosellas, Pennants, Mealy Rosellas, etc., is made thus: Get a piece of deal ⅝in. thick and 7ins. wide (a piece of 7-in. flooring will do). Cut off three lengths 16 inches long, for two sides and top, one 22 inches long for bottom, and two 6⅜ins. for the ends. Nail on one of the sides against the bottom, and the other side edge on to the bottom. The top will then be hinged to one side, and shut down on to the top of the other side, leaving the extra six inches of the bottom projecting for the birds to pitch upon when entering the nest. Fit in the two ends, first cutting a hole three inches in diameter near the top of the end which has the projecting piece at the bottom. One hinge to the top, if put in the centre, will be sufficient; the weight of the lid will keep it down without any fastening. This lid will be found very useful when cleaning out the nest, which cleaning will be needed before the young leave it.

If you should be fortunate and get five or six strong youngsters in one brood, as I have had many a time, they soon foul the nest, and, if allowed to get dirty, soon become sore on knees (or rather heels) and abdomen. When you have your box ready, put a layer of dry pine sawdust, about two inches deep, on the bottom of the box, pressing it well down, making a good cavity at the back for the reception of the eggs. See that there are no sharp-pointed bits of wood in the sawdust likely to prick through the shells of the eggs.

WHEN EGGS ARE LAID

After the first two or three eggs are laid it is best to look in before the hen commences to sit, to make sure that the sawdust is all right, and that the eggs are in a hollow together. Very few hens require much attention in this respect, except wild ones, which are apt to rush out of the nest at any sudden or unusual noise, and so scatter the eggs about the box. If the cock, however, goes into the box much, the sawdust may get levelled down.

The hen lays from three to seven white eggs rather smaller than a Pigeon's. Cockatiels generally begin to sit with about the third egg; sometimes with the first, and occasionally not until the last is laid. I say Cockatiels, for the cock sits by day and the hen by night. The hen (like the Budgerigar) lays on alternate days, so that when she commences to sit with the first egg, this means, if they all hatch, a considerable difference in the age and size of the young ones. But the smallest is very seldom injured by the others; and the parents seem to look after. the baby before its older brothers and sisters. I have frequently found the smallest with its crop almost bursting with food when the crops of the others seemed almost empty. Cockatiels sit about twenty days, and the young, when newly hatched, are covered with yellow, silky down.

THE USE OF BREAD.

Cockatiels are frugal feeders, and require nothing but Canary, white millet, and a few white oats. When they had young in the nest I at one time used a lot of bread for them, but I think it helps to foul the nest and keep the young very loose. Those who prefer to use bread (and some Cockatiels, if allowed, will feed their young almost entirely on it), should cut out a good piece of the crumb part of a stale loaf, and put it to soak in a bowl of cold water. After soaking ten or fifteen minutes, take it between the hands and squeeze as dry as possible, letting the water drain out between the fingers.

Cockatiels feed their young by taking their beaks inside their own (after the manner of Pigeons). Then with a pumping motion of the head the old birds bring the partly digested food from their crops into their beaks, from which the young ones feed.

COCKATOO OR PARRAKEET ?

This is another characteristic, besides the moving of the crest, which, in my humble opinion, brings the Cockatiel much nearer in relationship to the Cockatoos. For among all the Parrakeets I am acquainted with (such as Rosellas, Mealy Rosellas, Ringnecks, Plumheads, Pennants, Redrumps, Budgerigars, Kings, Bloodwings), every one I can call to mind, without exception, brings the food from the crop first into the beak, and then feeds, whereas Cockatoos (at least the Rose-breasted, which I have kept in my aviaries in pairs), feed like Cockatiels, viz., take the beak of the young in their own and then pump the food from the crop. Macaws feed in the same way as Parrakeets. I have put Rosellas' eggs under Cockatiels, which hatched them all right, but although the young Rosellas stayed in the nest three days, there was never a particle of food in their crops. Whether the Cockatiels knew they were not their own progeny, or whether they could not feed them, I am unable to say. Certain it is young Cockatiels in the same nest were well fed and all reared. I think these variations in the manner of feeding the young in different birds have not had the attention they deserve from aviculturists.

HATCHING AND REARING.

But to return to our subject. Cockatiels will breed at an age of twelve months, and have three and sometimes four broods in the season. I prefer, however, a two-year-old cock, for the younger ones will sometimes take no notice whatever of the eggs, and as the hen usually leaves them in the morning (thinking she has done her share), of course the eggs get spoilt when the cock shirks his task in the daytime, preferring to sit dozing beside his wife on the roost. The latter the hen soon finds out, but how she can tell there is no life in the eggs is a mystery. Still, when such is the case, the hens scarcely ever sit their time out, but commence to lay again after about ten or fourteen days. This is very annoying, as you cannot very well tell the difference between the newly-laid ones and the spoilt ones.

The young birds leave the nest when about five weeks old, and seldom return to it again. They are able to pick up food at about six weeks, though it is hardly safe to take them away at that age, for the old ones will continue to feed them for three months, or until there is another family to attend to.

If you desire to rear some that will be very tame, it is a good plan to put them in a Parrot cage a day or two after they leave the nest, and let the old ones tend them through the wires, putting soaked seed and water in the cage as well. The cage must be wired wide enough to allow the young ones or the parent birds to easily put their heads between the wires. This method will prevent them from getting as wild as they would do if allowed to have the fly of a large aviary.

Don't forget to give some cuttlefish bone or crushed egg-shells, or both, when your birds are going to nest, otherwise you will get soft-shelled eggs and egg bound hens, though these birds seem much freer from the latter complaint than Budgerigars. A little fresh groundsel may also be given, but do not let it stay in the aviary and get stale (or let the soaked bread go sour), or you will soon have no Cockatiels left to feed.

If fairly fortunate you will now have your young ones out of the nest and able to feed themselves, so I will devote a few remarks to taming them and teaching them to talk. Let me say at once that anyone who has a tame, talking male Cockatiel is to be envied, for such birds are the most delightful pets imaginable.

TO DISTINGUISH THE YOUNG MALES.

We will assume that we have secured our nest of young ones fully fledged and able to take care of themselves. Now we want to pick out our young cocks, either to tame and teach ourselves, or to sell for someone else to teach. This picking out of the young cocks is rather difficult, especially to a novice, for all the young resemble the mother.

I have seen the plucking of a few face feathers recommended, but this is not a bit of use. I once had nineteen young Cockatiels which left the nests at about the same time. When fully fledged, from each one I gently extracted a few feathers from the right-hand side of the face, leaving a very small bare spot. Here the plumage should have been renewed with yellow in the cock birds if this plan was a success, but the feathers came again on all of them the same colour as before. Further, strange though it may seem, when they moulted they did not shed the new feathers, and the cocks (there were twelve out of nineteen) when twelve months old, still had this little drab spot on the right-hand side of their yellow faces.

I find the best plan is to pick out the birds showing the brightest yellow tinge on the face, with the reddest earmarks, darkest and least-marked under side of tail, and with the boldest appearance about the head. If you do this, you will be pretty sure to spot the cock birds, although an experienced eye can usually pick out cocks from hens among birds which in plumage are exactly alike.

THE ART OF TAMING.

After selecting your birds, cage them separately, and the cocks will begin to warble and whistle about two or three weeks afterwards. Now is the time to commence taming operations, for they will have got used to their cages, and will be fairly quiet, providing they have not been roughly handled or frightened. Everyone who keeps birds should acquire the habit of moving gently when doing anything to or near them. Especially is this so when the taming or training of a bird is in question, for one sudden movement may undo what it has cost hours and perhaps days to accomplish. Remember, as the song says, "Gently does the trick." The following instructions will be found useful to anyone who has bought a young Cockatiel or other Parrakeet, to tame, as well as to the breeders of same. My plan, which is so successful that I have kept it a secret for many years, finding it so very remunerative, is this:—

THE FIRST LESSON.

Have the bird in a cage with the door large enough for you to put your hand in and out of it easily, and with the roost so fixed that it is easy to touch the bird's head. A square Parrot-cage is best, with the roost from side to side, so that the bird will face the door. In the evening, when the bird is asleep, turn the gas or lamp down very low, so that you can only just see the bird. Then begin talking to him gently, calling him by his name, generally "Joey," if a Cockatiel. Say "Pretty Joey," "Joey's a pretty bird," etc., in a coaxing tone, gently opening the cage door the while.

This will attract his attention, but if he be in any way frightened at this stage, when just awake, he will simply bang himself recklessly about the cage for ten minutes or so, screeching all the time, and he must be left alone for the rest of that night. Hence the necessity for being gentle.

If not frightened, your bird will now be on the watch, wondering what is going to happen. Pass your hand very slowly into the cage and above the bird's head, the palm being just above the top, so that your fingers will be in the right position to touch his poll just behind the crest. All this must be done so slowly that the bird does not notice the movement of your hand in the dark. Don't forget to repeat the above words to him while this is going on. Being unable to discern anything in the dark, his whole attention will be given to listening most intently.

KEEP ON TICKLING.

After waiting a minute, so that he will think everything is

all right, with one finger, or rather with your forefinger nail, lightly touch his poll feathers. He will, no doubt, start and bob his head when first touched, but you must keep your hand perfectly still until he is again settled. Then touch him once again. He will now probably make a hissing noise, and peck forward savagely, but, finding nothing in front, is doubtless a bit puzzled. After two or three such attempts the bird will remain quiet, and let you gently tickle his poll. Here ends his first lesson.

EXPOSE YOUR HAND.

When he appears to like having his poll tickled, or scratched, get someone to turn the gas or lamp up a little higher while you are doing it, so that he can just see your hand. After he is quiet, and you are still tickling his poll, raise the light still more; then gently take your hand away, but not out of the cage. Then quietly lift your hand over his head again, moving your finger as if scratching. He may peck at you a time or two, but you need not be afraid, for Cockatiels will not hurt unless handled, and then if you do not take hold of them the right way they will very soon take hold of you; yes, and let you know it, too. When your hand is over his head, he will put his head down a little. Now is the time to tickle him again.

When this lesson is over, have the light turned full on while he is quiet and you are scratching his poll. Then draw your hand gently out of the cage. This should have occupied you about an hour. Repeat this for a night or two, and he will have lost all fear of your hand. Then, when he will allow you to put your hand into his cage with the light full on and scratch his poll without showing any fear, you may try him in the daytime, but not before. I have had birds that I could do anything with by gaslight which were very timid in the daytime, My old Toucan for twelve months would allow me to scratch his poll or stroke him by gaslight, and seemed to enjoy it, yet would not let me put my hand near him by daylight.

THE LAST STAGE.

When your Cockatiel will allow you to scratch his poll in the daytime, put your hand in the cage and go through the motions of scratching with your finger about two inches in the front of him, and he will put his head down and advance that much to have it done. You can then soon get him to put his head through the wires, or come to the cage door, or even step out on to your finger, to get his poll scratched, for with most of the Parrot and Parrakeet tribe this seems their greatest enjoyment. You now have your bird perfectly tame, and with a little coaxing he will fly from his cage and pitch on your fingers. In fact, you can now do practically as you like with him, and you have one of the most delightful pets imaginable.

SENTENCES SOON LEARNT.

A few sentences that Cockatiels learn very quickly and distinctly are "Pretty Joey," "Kiss pretty," "Joey's a beauty," "Joey wants to come out," "Let poor Joe out," "Joey wants a biscuit" (but he generally says "Kiscuit" at first). Every time you go to his cage repeat distinctly what you want him to learn. One sentence at a time, however, or he will get them all mixed up together, such as "Joey's a kiss pretty," "Kiss pretty's a beauty." When you are teaching a bird to talk, you should always speak as though you were the bird and the bird were the master or mistress. Then when he has learnt his lessons it will appear as if he is talking to you, not merely repeating what he has learnt. Many people overlook this when teaching a Parrot.

GOOD WHISTLERS SHAKE THEIR HEADS.

If you want your Cockatiel to whistle a tune (and they are good whistlers), whistle clearly and distinctly what you want them to learn. If you have two or three in separate cages, sit down and whistle a lively air to them. Watch them carefully, and you will probably see one or two of them, after listening very attentively for a minute or two, shake their heads. Pick out those that shake their heads, for they will learn to whistle a tune in half the time the others will. I had one that learned to whistle the "Sailor's Hornpipe" right through, and dance on the roost to his own whistling; and this when only nine months old. The bird was kept in a back kitchen, where I always washed my hands on coming home to meals, and I whistled the ditty while doing so. Now, in a fortnight from commencing this the bird had made a start, and as soon as I entered the house would go through the first two bars without waiting for me to begin.

PARROT OWNERS, NOTE!

I may say, in conclusion, that owners of Grey Parrots may try the same method of taming their birds, for there is no bird more fond of having its poll scratched than "Polly." If they won't allow you to do this, it is only because they are afraid of your hand and bite at you in self defence.

9924128R00042

Printed in Great Britain
by Amazon.co.uk, Ltd.,
Marston Gate.